HALIMA SPEAKS

With love

DENISE EJOH PHD

Oct 2025

HALIMA SPEAKS

Denise Uzoma Ejoh, PhD

For permission requests or further information, contact:

Denise Ejoh, PhD

deniseejoh@me.com

First Edition

Printed in United Kingdom

Publisher National Library of Nigeria (NLN)

978-978-695-731-9

This book is dedicated to all metastatic breast cancer patients and their families for the prayers, love, patience, and encouragement given during the journey. We fight because you give us a shoulder to lean on.

Forward

Some stories are not just meant to be read; they are meant to be carried. This is one of them.

I met the author in 2010 when we were teaching, she taught Maths, and I taught English. But our bond quickly went beyond classrooms. We shared a fierce dedication to education and a deep passion for noticing and nurturing the hidden potential in students. That shared mission birthed a lasting friendship, even when life took us in different directions, she returned to Nigeria, and I moved on to other schools.

That same heart for impact beats through this book. She tells the story of a remarkable Nigerian woman on a mission to break the silence around cancer. This woman tireless, bold and compassionate gives voice to women, girls, and even men who would otherwise suffer in silence. Because of her work, fear gives way to hope, early detection becomes possible, and lives are saved.

The story is even more powerful because the author herself is a cancer survivor. She has and continues to walk the road of fear, endure the fight, and emerges with the gift of a second chance. That she would choose to turn that pain into purpose, and to shine a light for others, speaks volumes of her courage.

This book moved me deeply. It is about bravery, healing, community, and the unstoppable ripple effect of one person's determination.

To my dear friend, thank you for your strength, your compassion and your unwavering drive to lift others. This book is your legacy. And it is a blessing to us all.

Mrs Sevilley Johnson

Headteacher, Educator and Carer

United Kingdom

Halima Speaks

Contents

CHAPTER 1: Roots in the Dust

In the heart of Northern Nigeria, where the harmattan wind sweeps across red earth and the call to prayer rises with the sun, lived a woman whose presence echoed like folklore named Halima. Her name carried weight in the community, not because she sought attention, but because her life was a quiet storm of purpose.

Halima was born into a world of contrasts. Her mother, a calm, cocoa-skinned woman from Zaria, wore her *gele* like a crown and moved with the grace of a Fulani matron. Her father, a British-trained civil servant with a penchant for pepper soup and highlife music, brought his own flair to the family tree. The blend of cultures wasn't always seamless. Being mixed-race in Northern Nigeria had its own set of unwritten rules. As a child, Halima often found herself in-between too "light" for some, too "African" for others. But from that in-between, she carved out a fierce identity rooted in dignity and compassion.

Her childhood was embroidered with traditional festivals, long market days, and the thick smell of *tuwo shinkafa* (Ground rice balls) cooking over open flames. She grew up to the rhythm of Hausa proverbs and the steady beat of talking drums, understanding early that identity was not in the bloodline but in how one lived, loved, and gave.

By the time she settled in Minna, Halima had blossomed into more than just a woman of mixed heritage she was a community pillar. A devoted educator, she stood at the head of her classroom with a chalk in one hand and determination in the other. Her students were more than names on a register; they were seeds she tended to daily. As a mother of five, she juggled report cards and *mosque runs*, PTA meetings and market haggles, bedtime stories and moonlight tales. Her home was a haven where discipline danced with laughter, and prayer met play.

The Minna community knew her not only as "Madam Halima" but as a woman who showed up. She was the one who stayed after school to tutor the struggling girl from the outskirts. The woman who coordinated neighbourhood clean-ups during Sallah. The friend who always had *zobo* and wisdom ready, no matter the hour. She lived fully, like the sun before dusk, unapologetically warm and unwavering.

But even the sun hides behind clouds.

The signs came like whispers. A cough that lingered a bit too long. An ache in her back she chalked up to age and carrying her youngest on her hip. Fatigue that no afternoon nap could fix. In the busyness of life, she waved them away. What Northern woman paused for pain? Life was hard, yes but it had always been. You push. You pray. You press on.

Then came *that* moment. The one that divides life into "before" and "after." It was an evening like many others she was preparing dinner; her hands covered in *yaji*-spiced flour as she fried *masa*. Suddenly, she clutched her side, her breath catching. The pain wasn't new, but this time it stole her voice. Her daughter found her, eyes glazed with worry, and the family moved quickly from kitchen warmth to the cold walls of the hospital.

A scan. A biopsy. A doctor who paused too long before speaking.

Cancer.

The word fell like dust in her lungs, heavy and choking. She had spent years caring for others, breathing life into classrooms, stories, and children. Now, her own breath was being taken.

But Halima, raised in red earth, shaped by tradition, steeled by faith did not crumble. Her journey had just turned, yes, but the roots were deep. The roots, as always, were in the ground. The first time Halima looked at herself in the mirror after her hair began to fall out, she froze. It wasn't vanity it was the shock of unfamiliarity. The strong, vibrant woman who had once knotted her *gele* with pride and stepped into her classroom like a general, now stared back with hollow eyes and thinning eyebrows. She wrapped her scarf tighter, not just for modesty, but for strength. In Northern culture, head coverings were normal, but now, hers felt like armour.

There was no roadmap for what she was going through. In Minna, cancer still lived in whispers. People spoke of it only when someone died. The idea of surviving, of fighting, enduring, was rarely part of the narrative. And yet, here she was, in the thick of it.

Her days followed a new routine: early morning prayers, followed by medication. Some days, she felt strong enough to help the younger ones with their schoolwork or sit outside in the compound and listen to the birds. On others, the pain was too sharp, the fatigue too thick. She would lie in bed, the *adire* cloth pulled over her legs, her Qur'an resting beside her, a quiet companion.

The chemo sessions stripped her physically, but they revealed a deeper, quieter strength. She began journaling, something she'd never done before. At first, they were just scribbles: verses, prayers, names of those who visited. But slowly, they became reflections. She wrote about her fears, yes, but also about gratitude. She wrote about the joy in seeing her youngest son fall asleep beside her without fear. About her daughter learning how to cook *miyan taushe* (Pumpkin Stew) just the way she liked it. About the neighbour who brought fresh *kunu* (Tiger Nut Milk) every Tuesday, without fail.

Her illness, in its strange way, began to pull people closer.

Faith played an even deeper role now. She'd always been devout, but now her conversations with God were more intimate. She prayed not just for healing, but for understanding, for the strength to carry the weight of uncertainty. Her tasbih became a lifeline, each bead a quiet surrender.

The mosque community organized special prayers. Women visited with their own stories, some had lost sisters or mothers to the same disease, some were surviving it silently. These visits birthed a hidden sisterhood. Halima learned how many women in her community were quietly carrying their own burdens, undiagnosed, untreated, unseen. Together, they began to speak more openly. Not loudly, but boldly. Cancer, they agreed, could no longer be a taboo.

And then came the question she hadn't yet faced head-on.

"Mummy are you going to die?" her eight-year-old son asked one night, his voice barely above a whisper.

She pulled him close. Her body ached, her mouth was dry, but her words were steady.

"I don't know, my love. But I know I'm still here today. And I'll be here tomorrow. And we'll keep walking, together."

In that moment, she realized what this battle truly meant not just surviving, but living, day by day, with grace and courage. And even in her quietest moments, even when her strength was drained and her body rebelled, her spirit never bowed.

The battle had begun, yes but, so had a transformation.

Cancer was a thief. It stole time, comfort, and the warm rhythm of normalcy. But in its theft, it revealed life's hidden treasures, zobo at sunset, a whispered prayer, the light in her daughter's eyes as she stirred the soup just right.

Some still believed cancer was a curse, or the price for unseen sins. Others thought it meant certain death. But Halima refused to carry that silence."

In the land of red dust and quiet faith, Halima's story would not end in whispers it would rise like the call to prayer, reminding all who heard it that even in illness, there is life.

CHAPTER 2: The Quiet Battle Begins

The news rippled through Halima's household like hot oil dropped into cold water - sharp, sizzling, and sudden.

Cancer.

A word people in Minna didn't say out loud. They would rather whisper *"wata cuta mai muni"* (bad illness or a terrible disease) that terrible sickness or simply shake their heads and say, *"Allah ya tsare."* (May Allah protect). In many homes, the word itself was taboo, like calling the devil by name.

Halima sat on her prayer mat that night, the doctor's words ringing louder than the adhan. Not just "you have cancer," but that second blow

"We caught it late."

That part hit her harder than the diagnosis.

She sat still, tasbih beads slipping through her fingers slowly, lips moving in prayer, but her heart replayed every moment she had ignored the signs.

That cough that danced around like it owned her chest.

The back pain that refused to go even after Fati's strong balm and her neighbour's "guaranteed" shea butter and ginger mix.

The fatigue that followed her like her shadow.

But how could she have known? Was she not a mother of five, a teacher, a community woman? Who had time to complain of tiredness when *life itself na marathon*?

Musa, her husband, was quiet. Too quiet.

A man of few words, now reduced to even fewer. When the doctor had spoken, Musa didn't ask a single question. He just stood with his cap in his hand, eyes downcast, nodding slightly as if someone had just priced his best goat too low.

Since then, he'd taken up duties like he was preparing for an exam: driving her to the hospital, reminding her of her medicine, blending papaya and moringa with the seriousness of a pharmacist. But affection? That was harder. Like many Northern men, he showed love with action, not with words.

So instead of "I'm scared," he said:

"Halima, I've told Sani to slaughter that big cock for you. You need strength."

She smiled faintly.

Typical Musa. Always offering protein when it was comfort that was needed.

The children reacted in their own ways. Maryam, the eldest, started acting like the junior matron of the house writing down mummy's medicine times in a notebook and rearranging the kitchen like it was her own chemist.

Sadiq, the second, took it upon himself to "Google" everything.

"Mummy, this one says you should drink bitter leaf water mixed with coconut oil and turmeric before sunrise."

"And after that should I also fly to the moon?" Halima teased weakly.

The younger ones, Salma, Idris, and baby Fatima hovered close. Clingy. Asking questions that twisted her heart.

“Is cancer like a cough?”

“Will it go away with paracetamol?”

“Will Mummy be bald like Baba Musa’s head?”

She would laugh, a small, tired laugh, not because it was funny, but because laughter was one of the few thing’s cancers hadn’t touched yet.

Then chemo began.

She hated that place.

The white walls, the sharp smell of spirits and rubber gloves, the air too cold even for harmattan standards. She used to come here once to give health talks to mothers. Now she sat among the same patients, holding her stomach, trying to smile through the nausea.

She named the chemo chair “kujerar jarumta”, the warrior’s throne. Not because she felt strong, but because sitting in it meant she had shown up again. And sometimes, just showing up was enough.

Some days, she came home with the taste of iron in her mouth and the mood of a wet cat. Food disgusted her. Even the aroma of her beloved miyan taushe now smelled like burnt tyres.

“Mummy, should I still cook rice?” Maryam would ask.

"Cook it. Whether I eat it or stare at it, it's still better than hospital drip."

They laughed. Laughed at nothing. Laughed at the way her eyebrows were disappearing like a thief in the night.

"Ehn ehn, so cancer has manners? It started with hair, then came for the brows?"

"Before it takes my eyelashes, let me at least bat my eyes at Musa one last time."

The hospital, once a place she visited with students for health talks, was now a second home. The smell of antiseptic. The sterile silence. The faint beeping of monitors. These became her new soundtrack. Each session took a piece of her - **her hair**, her strength, her taste for food but also gifted her clarity.

There were days she couldn't get out of bed. Days her body revolted against her, where nausea and weakness became her morning prayers. And yet, she rose maybe not every morning, but enough to show her family that the fight was still on.

Outside, the world remained itself.

Children still chased tyres down dusty streets.

Mama Yakubu still shouted at customers in the market,

"If you no get money, shift! Onions no be charity!"

And of course, word had spread.

"Madam Halima... She gets that sickness."

"Ahn ahn! But she dey look normal o!"

"Abeg (please), make person no go catch am."

Ignorance wore many wrappers.

Still, some showed up. Women from the mosque brought soups in warm flasks and stories to make her laugh. Her neighbour, Aunty Jummai, came every Tuesday with kunu and gossip.

"You hear say that Hajiya's son finally married that Lagos girl?"

*"After all her English, she still no sabi (*doesn't know*) cook tuwo (*swallow*). Hmmm, this generation."*

And Halima would laugh, her chest rising painfully, but still laughing.

Her former students returned some now tall boys with deep voices and buba too big for their frames coming to recite Qur'an with her and sit in silence when words failed.

But it wasn't always laughter.

There were days the body refused to move. Days the prayer mat stayed empty because the pain was too sharp. Days she held the Qur'an not to read but to simply feel its presence beside her.

She started writing. Scribbles at first. Prayers. Names. Verses.

Then thoughts.

"Today, my eyes are yellow. But my heart is calm."

"Maryam made tea and forgot the sugar. I drank it like it was nectar."

"Musa tried to plait Fatima's hair. I have never seen such disaster."

Cancer stole many things, but somehow, it gave space to see clearly.

She saw love in the way her daughter sat by her feet.

She saw loyalty in the quiet hospital driver who never once complained about delays.

She saw God in the smallest things, a breeze through her window, a bird perching on the mango tree, the silence between two beads of her tasbih.

The community rallied. Quietly at first. Then with boldness.

The mosque held special prayers.

A few women began to speak up too gently, but firmly.

Halima had become the unspoken leader of a new kind of group: women who refused to suffer in silence.

One whispered,

"Wallahi, my sister died like this. She no tell anybody."

Another added,

"I dey feel lump too, but na you give me courage to go hospital."

They weren't making noise. But they were making change.

Outside, the world continued its rhythm. The call to prayer still echoed through Minna at dawn. Children still laughed on dusty playgrounds. Women still gathered at the market, bargaining over okra and onions. But word had spread.

"Madam Halima has cancer," they whispered.

Some avoided her, unsure of what to say or afraid it was contagious, as ignorance sometimes leads people to believe. But others showed up. Women from the mosque brought soups and *kunun gyada (*hausa-fulani meal made from groundnut*)*. Neighbours took turns escorting her to the hospital. Former students came to read to her and pray with her.

And for the first time, Halima saw what she had built. All those years of service, kindness, and community were not forgotten. Her life, it seemed, had planted seeds far wider than she realized. And now, in her most vulnerable moment, those seeds were blooming.

Cancer had come, yes. But so had strength.

Not the loud kind with fists in the air, but the quiet kind. The kind that shows up to appointments when you'd rather sleep. The kind that lets your child see you bald and still smile. The kind that whispers, "We keep going."

The quiet battle had begun. And Halima, as always, would face it on her own terms with faith in her heart, fire in her spirit, and her roots, still firm, in the dust.

The first time Halima looked at herself in the mirror after her hair began to fall out, she froze. It wasn't vanity, it was the shock of unfamiliarity. The strong, vibrant woman who had once knotted her *gele* with pride and stepped into her classroom like a general, now stared back with hollow eyes and thinning eyebrows. She wrapped her scarf tighter, not just for modesty, but for strength. In Northern culture, head coverings were normal, but now, hers felt like armour.

There was no roadmap for what she was going through. In Minna, cancer still lived in whispers. People spoke of it only when someone died. The idea of surviving, of fighting, enduring, was rarely part of the narrative. And yet, here she was, in the thick of it.

Her days followed a new routine: early morning prayers, followed by medication. Some days, she felt strong enough to help the younger ones with their schoolwork or sit outside in the compound and listen to the birds. On others, the pain was too sharp, the fatigue too thick. She would lie in bed, the *adire* cloth pulled over her legs, her Qur'an resting beside her, a quiet companion.

The chemo sessions stripped her physically, but they revealed a deeper, quieter strength. She began journaling, something she'd never done before. At first, they were just scribbles: verses, prayers, names of those who visited. But slowly, they became reflections. She wrote about her fears, yes, but also about gratitude. She wrote about the joy in seeing her youngest son fall asleep beside her without fear. About her daughter learning how to cook *miyan taushe* just the way she liked it. About the neighbour who brought fresh *kunu* every Tuesday, without fail.

Her illness, in its strange way, began to pull people closer.

Faith played an even deeper role now. She'd always been devout, but now her conversations with God were more intimate. She prayed not just for healing, but for understanding for the strength to carry the weight of uncertainty. Her tasbih became a lifeline, each bead a quiet surrender.

The mosque community organized special prayers. Women visited with their own stories some had lost sisters or mothers to the same disease, some were surviving it silently. These visits birthed a hidden sisterhood. Halima learned how many women in her community were quietly carrying their own burdens undiagnosed, untreated, unseen. Together, they began to speak more openly. Not loudly, but boldly. Cancer, they agreed, could no longer be a taboo.

Then came that one question.

One night, Idris, her eight-year-old, climbed into bed and asked,

"Mummy… are you going to die?"

Her body hurt. Her lips were dry. But her words were full.

"I don't know, my love. But I'm still here today. I'll be here tomorrow. We'll keep walking, *wallahi*. Together."

He nodded, sniffed, and rested his head on her arm.

And in that moment, with one child's breath against her skin and the pain thrumming in her bones, Halima knew:

This wasn't about just surviving.

It was about living. With grace. With humour. With her roots still in the dust.

Cancer had come, yes.

But it had not taken her.

CHAPTER 3: From Silence to Strength

In Northern Nigerian culture, illness, especially cancer is often spoken about in hushed tones, as if naming it gives it power. Halima had once accepted that silence. But now, sitting in hospital corridors alongside women who stared at their hands instead of each other, she began to see the cost of that quiet. Too many women came in late. Too many left too soon. All because fear and shame had muted their voices.

Halima had always been a teacher. Now, she realized she was still teaching just from a different classroom.

One morning, while waiting for her consultation, she leaned toward a woman who looked just like her: scarf tied tight, eyes tired, hands trembling slightly.

“You’re not alone,” Halima said gently.

The woman looked up, startled. And then, her shoulders softened. That small exchange sparked something. Word spread in the hospital about the teacher with cancer who wasn't afraid to talk. Nurses began pointing newly diagnosed women her way. Sometimes she just sat with them. Sometimes she prayed. Sometimes, she simply listened.

Her living room turned into a quiet gathering space. What began as tea with a neighbour became regular sit-downs with women from across Minna, some diagnosed, some just afraid.

They asked questions she once didn't know how to answer: *What does chemotherapy feel like? Will my husband still look at me the same? Can I still be a mother, a wife, a woman?*

Halima didn't pretend to have all the answers. But she shared her truth. She spoke of the night she cried into her prayer mat, of the shame she felt watching her children care for her, of the freedom that came when she accepted help without guilt.

The conversations grew. Slowly, courage blossomed. One woman brought her sister to be screened. Another spoke at her women's cooperative. Halima saw it happen, one voice at a time, the silence was cracking.

By the end of the year, with encouragement from her daughter and former students, Halima partnered with a local clinic to organize "**Women of Strength**", a small, informal program offering cancer education and screenings.

She couldn't attend every session, but her story was always part of the message. Her face head wrapped in a colourful *turban*, eyes kind but fierce became a quiet symbol of what was possible.

She was still fighting, of course. The road was not smooth. There were infections. Setbacks. Nights when she wondered if it was worth it. But each time a woman called her to say, "I got checked because of you," she found her second wind.

Chemo continues......

By the third round of chemotherapy, Halima could feel the shift not just in her bones, in her blood, in her now-brittle fingernails but in the secret corners of her mind. The weakness had become a familiar, uninvited roommate. She no longer flinched when her hair came out in strands on her pillow or when her mouth tasted like rust and burnt onions. Her body was now fluent in a strange new language a painful one, but it spoke of survival, of surrender, of fragile triumphs.

But deeper than the physical toll was the echo chamber in her head. Some nights, when the house had gone quiet and the moon sat softly above the guava tree, her thoughts would sneak in like uninvited relatives.

"Will my children remember me as I was… or as I am now?"

"Did I waste too much time ignoring myself?"

"If I die, who will help Musa remind Hassan to wear slippers outside?"

She would smile at that last thought through her tears. Even in darkness, motherhood clung like skin.

Her emotions were no longer neat. One minute she felt brave, a lioness in a wrapper. The next, she was weeping over the way Musa had arranged her medication tray like it was a sacred ritual. He never said much Northern men rarely did when it came to illness, but he was there. Sometimes that presence was enough. Other times, it was a silence she wanted to scream into.

"Ka ji Musa," she said one evening as he sat beside her during a power cut, fanning her slowly with a cardboard fan shaped like a mosque dome, "You've turned me into one big baby o. If I sneeze now, you'll call the pharmacist."

Musa chuckled under his breath. *"Allah ya sauwake* (God bless you), Halima. I prefer you laughing like this than sleeping like wood."

They both laughed. Not because the pain was gone, but because they had found small pockets of joy between the thorns.

But the mental weight lingered. The fear wasn't just about dying. It was about disappearing. About leaving no trace except folded wrappers in a cupboard and unpaid school fees. There were days she felt guilty for getting sick. Days she felt selfish for needing help. Days she couldn't pray without her mind spiralling into questions that had no answers.

Her teenage daughter, Maryam, once found her crying in the bathroom.

"Mama, are you okay?"

"*Na ji zafi* (I felt pain), baby," Halima said, wiping her eyes. "But don't worry. It's the kind that teaches you something."

Maryam didn't press further. She simply sat on the floor and painted her mother's toenails pink. A small rebellion against sorrow.

The weakness had become familiar now, a guest she no longer resisted. Her body was learning a new language of pain and recovery, of surrender and small victories. But something else was growing within her too something strong, urgent, and clear.

She had been quiet long enough.

The living room became a sanctuary of sorts. Old students dropped by with zobo and stories. A neighbour brought suya unasked. Even Musa's sister, who had once called cancer "the whisper of the grave," came to sit and plait Halima's hair - what was left of it with shaky fingers and apologies.

Still, not everyone understood.

One uncle had said flatly, "Why are you telling people about this thing? *E no good for family name.*" Another advised her to "just pray more, not talk too much." But Halima was tired of carrying her pain in silence. She wanted to **wear it**, not as shame, but as testimony.

So, she began to speak.

It started at home, during Maghrib prayers, when she gently corrected her children's whispers with the truth: "It's cancer. And no, it's not a curse." Then came the women's prayer group, where she finally shared her diagnosis and story not with pity, but with fire.

By the time she stood before the mosque women's circle that Friday, her voice was steadier than even she expected.

"*Wannan cuta ba ta tsani ka* - meaning this disease doesn't hate you. Cancer is not something we should fear like a jinn (a supernatural being) in the dark. It's something we fight. And we fight it better when we talk."

Her advocacy grew not because she shouted, but because her words carried weight. Women who had hidden their lumps, their bleeding, their shame began to speak. One brought her sister for screening. Another admitted she had been using herbs in secret but wanted to know if there was another way.

In a region where silence was often mistaken for strength, Halima's gentleness was a revolution.

Musa surprised her by building a shaded area in their compound with old mats and plastic chairs. "For your meeting," he said quietly. It became their "small clinic" where women could gather for tea, talk, prayer and courage.

At first, he simply sat in the back, watching. Eventually, he started helping organize transportation for rural women. Her eldest son designed flyers. Her youngest drew pictures of "Mummy the Brave" and taped them on the walls.

The illness had taken many things from her. But it had also revealed a purpose bigger than she imagined.

Her story was no longer just about survival. It was about shifting a culture. About showing that courage can live in weakness, that illness does not steal dignity, and that even in dust, roots can rise and bloom.

When Halima began speaking out, she didn't set out to become a symbol. She only wanted to make the silence less heavy for herself, and for women like her. But the silence was deep-rooted, embedded in generations of cultural reservation, fear, and misinformation.

Cancer, in her community, was more than a disease. It was a rumour, a shame, a sentence spoken only when the final breath had been taken. Women whispered it behind veils. Men changed the topic when it was mentioned. Even the word itself- *cancer* was foreign, clunky in the local dialect, carrying the weight of the unknown.

But Halima understood something now: fear thrives in darkness. And the only way to fight fear was to bring light.

She began by telling her story during Friday women's prayer gatherings. At first, it was just a few sentences shared during post-prayer chatter, but word spread quickly. "Halima is talking." "Halima is still alive." "Halima is helping others." That last one, it stuck. Helping others despite her illness, not after it.

One afternoon, as Halima sat beneath the tree with a group of women, her youngest, Aisha, ran out with a drawing.

It showed a stick-figure woman with a scarf, a big heart drawn in red, and the words "Super Mummy" written across the top in uneven letters.

"Why the big heart?" one of the women asked.

"Because her heart is still strong," Aisha said, proudly.

Halima blinked fast.

One of the boldest moves came during a women's event at the local mosque, where she was asked to speak. It was a risk. Many religious spaces were still uncomfortable with such discussions. But she stepped to the front, her frame visibly thinner, her scarf carefully tied to cover the baldness, her voice firm.

She didn't give a lecture.

She told a story.

She spoke of the first pain in her side, of the hospital corridors, of watching her hair fall out in clumps like feathers, of praying for her children's future when she wasn't sure she'd be in it.

She ended with a plea: "Go. Get checked. Talk to your daughters. Don't let silence take you before sickness does."

But the truth is, not every day was triumphant.

There were days when the house felt too loud, when her own body felt like betrayal. She would sit on her prayer mat and just breathe. No words. No verses. Just the rhythm of survival.

She journaled those days too.

"Today, the pain was worse than yesterday. But Fati made moi-moi without burning it. Victory."

"Today, I watched the rain fall and let it remind me: even the ground must cry sometimes."

The hall was still. Some wept openly. Others nodded silently, their own private battles reflected in her words. Afterward, women lined up not to ask questions but to thank her. One leaned in and whispered, "I found a lump. I've been afraid to tell anyone. But maybe… maybe it's not too late."

That evening, Halima sat quietly in her courtyard under the guava tree, watching the sky soften into dusk. Her husband joined her, carrying two cups of *kunu*. For a while, they said nothing. Then he reached for her hand.

"You're changing things," he said.

She looked at him and smiled, a weary but warm smile. 'I'm just telling the truth, "She replied.

Still, advocacy wasn't always welcomed.

Some family members discouraged her openness. "Why are you making this public? It's a private matter," an aunt had scolded. Others worried it would bring shame or pity. But Halima stood her ground. Shame had already stolen too many lives. Pity wasn't what she wanted awareness was.

Her children, once frightened by her fragility, now saw her differently. Her daughters began speaking about women's health in their school groups. Her sons, once unsure of how to approach her pain, now protected her with a tenderness that spoke volumes.

And in the city, people were beginning to take notice.

A local journalist reached out to profile her. A clinic in Abuja asked her to share her experience in a virtual panel. Suddenly, Halima's voice; the same voice that once whispered nursery rhymes to sleepy toddlers was being amplified across communities.

She started keeping a notebook titled "**Things They Should Know**." It was filled with scribbled thoughts, quotes, reminders. She didn't know what it would become a speech, a book, a legacy? But it was hers. Her voice, on paper.

One entry read:

"Cancer is not a punishment. It is a test. And like all tests, we are meant to learn something. About life. About love. About the power of truth."

That truth had given her a second life, not free of illness, but full of meaning.

She hadn't defeated cancer. But she had denied it the power to silence her. And in doing so, she gave her community, especially its women, permission to speak, to question, to seek help.

From silence to strength, from teacher to advocate, Halima was becoming more than her diagnosis.

She was becoming a movement.

Months passed. "**Women of Strength**" grew. A doctor from Kaduna offered to support their next screening event. Her story was published in a local Hausa newsletter. And yet, Halima remained deeply rooted. She was still a mother. A wife. A woman in battle.

But now, she was also a lighthouse.

And in her quiet way, she had lit a fire that could no longer be put out.

Cancer had taken her hair, her energy, parts of her identity.

But it had also given her vision. Purpose. And most of all, a voice strong enough to shake silence to its knees.

CHAPTER 4: The Echo Beyond Minna

Halima never sought to be seen.

Her life had been built on the invisible work of women like her greeting neighbours with kuli-kuli (groundnut snack) and kindness, teaching multiplication tables under the fan's slow sweep, praying silently for her family's wellbeing long after they had gone to sleep. She did not campaign for visibility; she carried her calling in whispers.

But now her story had gathered a sound too loud to ignore. And even as her body began to dim, her voice had found amplification in places she had never imagined.

In early November, a letter came from the **Federal College of Health Sciences in Dowa**. They wanted to name a lecture series after her. She blinked at the words, read them twice, then passed the letter to Musa in silence.

His hands trembled slightly as he read it. Then he looked at her with a face full of pride and worry.

"Halima, your name dey fly now like morning adhan. But your body…"

She nodded slowly. "I know, Musa. I feel it."

But she didn't stop.

She recorded a series of radio messages in Hausa simple, direct words for market women, farmers, schoolteachers.

Messages like: *"If your breast pains you and you are not breastfeeding, don't ignore it."* Or *"Our mothers suffered in silence, but we do not have to.* "She insisted the jingles end with this:

"This message is from Halima Yusuf. I am living with cancer. And I want you to live too."

The radio stations played it daily. Bus drivers left the volume up. A woman in a cotton kaftan heard one of the jingles, checked her symptoms, and got referred early. The doctors caught it in time. She later wrote to Halima, calling her "my voice in the dark."

But Halima's light was flickering.

She began to sleep more. Her laughter became quieter. The fatigue wasn't just from the treatment; it was from the toll of carrying so many hopes.

Zainab noticed it first.

"Mama, maybe this is the time to rest."

Halima smiled softly. "No, baby. This is the time to delegate."

And so, she did. Piece by piece, she handed over:

- The women's awareness circle in Minna was passed on to Aunty Bilkisu, who had once been afraid to even say the word "cancer."
- The outreach team in Suleja was now led by *Tijjani*, her former student, who had turned down a marketing job to work full-time on health education.
- The little awareness group that met under her mango tree every Thursday had now merged with a wider network of community health volunteers in the North Central.

She had built without blueprint. And now, others were building beside her.

One afternoon, the Minister for Women's Affairs visited Halima's home unannounced. No fanfare, no convoy just a single Hilux and a humble aide.

“I came to thank you,” the Minister said, standing in the shaded corner of Halima’s compound. “Your voice has done more than any campaign budget we’ve ever approved.”

Halima smiled weakly, her scarf slightly slipping as she tried to sit up straighter. “I’m just… a teacher,” she said.

“No,” the Minister replied. “You are a movement.”

That night, Halima sat on her porch wrapped in two shawls. It was cold. Harmattan had crept in. The sky above was wide and clear. Zainab brought her tea. It tasted like memory ginger, cloves, honey. She looked at her daughter and saw fire.

“Promise me something,” she said.

Zainab leaned in.

“If this story ends… don’t let the message die with me.”

Zainab didn’t cry. She nodded. A strong, stubborn nod. “It won’t.”

It began with an invitation one that came tucked inside a formal envelope with a golden crest, delivered by a courier who looked slightly confused to find himself in a compound lined with drying laundry and neighbourhood children playing football.

The National Health Advocacy Summit in Abuja had heard about her work - "grassroots cancer awareness pioneer," they called her. They wanted her to speak on a panel alongside medical professionals, policymakers, and NGO heads. Halima was stunned. She'd never stood on a stage like that. But her children wide-eyed and proud encouraged her.

"Mummy, they want your story," her daughter said. *"Not just your strength. Your truth."*

The journey to Abuja was long and tiring, and her body already fragile from months of treatment rebelled. She coughed often. Her appetite was poor. The fatigue came in waves, like thick fog. But her resolve was clear.

She walked into the conference hall dressed in a flowing *zanna bukar*, her scarf embroidered with tiny golden threads. Her gait was slower now, more deliberate. But when she stood before the microphone, the room leaned in.

Halima didn't speak in English for the first few minutes. She greeted them in Hausa. She spoke as a mother, as a teacher, as a woman who had watched her life unravel and reweave itself thread by thread.

"We do not fear what we understand," she said. *"But we fear cancer because no one talks about it. Because we wait until it's too late. Because we do not listen to the women who are dying silently."*

The hall was quiet. And then, the applause - thunderous, unrestrained. The kind that came not just from respect, but from recognition. Halima had said what many had been afraid to say.

After the event, she was approached by doctors, reporters, young activists. Her story was featured in national papers. A short documentary was made about her. Invitations followed from health foundations and international bodies. An NGO from the UK reached out to feature her in a global series on "Women Changing the Narrative on Cancer in Africa." Her image scarfed, smiling, resolute appeared alongside stories from Rwanda, India, and Brazil.

But while the world was celebrating her voice, her body was starting to falter.

One evening, after a long virtual session with a global health forum, she collapsed in her sitting room. Her son caught her just before her head hit the floor. It was an infection; her immunity was too weak. She was hospitalized for days, barely able to speak, her lungs heavy and her hands trembling.

Lying in the sterile white hospital bed, Halima faced the question again the one she thought she had already answered: What if I don't survive this?

And this time, she answered it differently.

She didn't just think of her children, her husband, her students.

She thought of the woman in a remote village who might feel a lump but stay silent out of fear. The teenage girl who heard her mother's story and decided to become a nurse. The imam who allowed cancer screenings in the mosque courtyard after hearing Halima speak. She thought of her notebook "Things They Should Know"- and the fact that people were reading it now, not just in Minna, but across the country.

She may not control how long she lived. But she had already shaped what she would leave behind.

When she was discharged weeks later, weaker but breathing easier, the community gathered outside her home. There were prayer chants, songs, gifts. The local government named her a Community Health Ambassador. A mural was painted in her honour on the wall of the hospital she once feared entering.

Global recognition had come, yes. But it was the little things, the softened hearts, the opened conversations, the daughters walking their mothers to clinics that mattered most.

In bed that night, her youngest son asked, “Mummy, are you still fighting?”

She smiled and pulled him close.

“Always,” she said. “But now I’m not fighting alone.”

Halima had always believed that a whisper could grow into a wave if carried by the right winds. But even she hadn’t imagined how far her voice would travel.

What began as a quiet movement in Minna, born out of hospital benches, prayer circles, and backyard gatherings was now crossing borders, both literal and symbolic.

Her message was simple, but radical in its context: *Cancer is not a curse. It is not a taboo. It is a call to act, early, boldly, and together.*

It was during a local community outreach in Suleja that the call came a producer from the Federal Ministry of Health wanted to include Halima in a keynote panel for the National Women's Health Policy Dialogue in Abuja. "You're changing the landscape," the caller said. "We need your voice in the room."

Halima was honoured. But her body reminded her of its limits. She had begun to feel dizzy spells and chest pressure. Her oncologist urged her to rest.

But she went.

Abuja was different from Minna, wide roads, suited officials, cameras. The hall was filled with scholars, NGO heads, dignitaries, health ministers. At first, she felt out of place in her richly embroidered *abada*, worn modestly but proudly. Then she looked down at the notes in her lap, the story of a woman who almost didn't survive because nobody talked and she stood up to speak.

"Cancer is not just cells misbehaving in our bodies," she said. *"It is silence eating through our communities. It is shame disguised as tradition. It is a mother who finds a lump and waits, because she doesn't know she's allowed to ask."*

Gasps. Nods. A woman in the third row clutched her chest. Journalists raised their cameras. By the time she finished, the hall gave her a standing ovation.

Afterward, a British health foundation approached

her about partnering for a cross-continental awareness campaign. An editor from Daily Trust asked for an exclusive feature. Social media buzzed with hashtags: #HalimaSpeaks #NorthernVoicesForHealth #BreakTheSilence.

International recognition followed. The Global Alliance for Women's Health awarded her a Certificate of Impact. She was invited to share a pre-recorded message at the **Geneva Global Health Forum**. A Nigerian ambassador abroad quoted her speech during a policy session in Brussels.

Her children watched in awe as their mother's name filled newspapers and television scrolls. "Halima Yusuf, advocate, educator, survivor."

But just as her voice was becoming a national anthem of hope, her body began to fail her again.

One evening, after returning from a live radio interview, Halima collapsed beside her bed. Her youngest daughter screamed. Musa rushed in from the kitchen. Her breathing was shallow, her skin clammy. She was rushed to the hospital, where doctors confirmed a serious chest infection. Her immune system, battered from cycles of chemotherapy and stress, was too weak to fight it alone.

A week later, Halima's voice faded into sleep.

Not dramatically. Not with hospital machines or headlines. She died at dawn, in her own bed, with Musa beside her holding her hand, whispering *Al-Fātiḥah*. Her last breath came soft, like a feather falling from a hen's wing.

Word spread fast. But there were no sirens, no funeral crowds in designer lace. Her burial followed the quiet rites of her faith. Dust to dust. Prayers in soft voices. Children watching, unsure what it all meant.

But something began that day.

A candlelight walk was held in Abuja initiated by cancer survivors who never met her but knew her voice.

A panel at the Geneva Women's Health Forum opened with a tribute video of Halima's speeches in Hausa, subtitled for a world that finally cared to listen.

In Minna, at the same hospital where she was once afraid to enter, a new wing was announced:

The Halima Yusuf Centre for Women's Health and Early Detection.

The plaque at the entrance read:

"Because she spoke, we now listen. Because she lived, we live better."

Her notebook, **Things They Should Know**, was published posthumously. The first print sold out within two weeks. The foreword was written by Zainab, who had inherited not just her mother's name, but her mantle.

At a girls' secondary school in Sokoto, students recite parts of Halima's speech during assembly.

In Lokoja, a young nurse runs a podcast called **The Daughter of Halima** - where women tell stories of illness, healing, silence, and voice.

In Gombe, a widowed tailor named Amina teaches her apprentices how to feel for breast lumps.

And in Abuja, a little girl pointed to Halima's mural and said, "That's the woman who told mummy to go to the clinic."

A mural painted on the side of the community clinic: Halima in her signature scarf, surrounded by silhouettes of women standing tall, hand in hand. Below it, a quote:

"We speak because silence is no longer an option."

Her impact had outgrown her voice.

The echo had travelled.

Beyond Minna.

Beyond markets and mosques.

Beyond borders.

Halima never made it to Geneva. But Geneva now knows her name.

And so do we.

She had become more than a survivor. She had become a structure. A seed planted in truth, watered by courage, and growing now wild and wide.

CHAPTER 5: The Voice on the Screen

The first time Halima saw her face on television; she was seated on the same couch where she had once wept silently after her diagnosis.

Now, her face filled the screen bright, wrapped in a soft lilac *gele*, her voice calm and steady. The banner read:

"Courage and Cancer: A Conversation with Halima Yusuf."

What began as whispered conversations in living rooms and mosque courtyards had now found a new home: the screen. And with it, Halima had found an entirely new classroom.

It started with a producer from the Northern-based station Arewa Sunrise TV, who had watched her speak at the Abuja Summit. He reached out with an idea: a television series short, culturally rooted episodes tackling the stigma around cancer, highlighting real stories, and educating women across Nigeria in the language they understood best.

Halima was hesitant. She wasn't an actress or a presenter. But the producer had one line that stayed with her:

"You don't need to act, Hajia. Just be yourself. Be the woman who already saved lives without a camera."

The program launched three months later under the title "Halima Speaks: Truth, Health, and Hope." Each 30-minute episode was filmed in Hausa, laced with proverbs, music, and warmth that reflected the traditions of the North. It didn't look like a typical health show it looked like a gathering under a mango tree. But it carried weight.

Halima spoke directly to viewers. She invited doctors and survivors. She answered anonymous questions sent in by women who couldn't ask their husbands or imams. She toured local markets, asking women if they knew what a breast lump felt like. She laughed with them, cried with them, prayed with them.

One segment showed her explaining chemotherapy using millet grains. Another had her seated with a Fulani woman who traveled five hours to share her story of survival. Every episode ended the same way with Halima looking straight into the camera and saying:

"Speak. Ask. Listen. *You are not alone."*

The impact was immediate.

Rural women gathered around small TVs and battery-powered radios to tune in. Calls flooded the studio. Clinics saw an uptick in early-stage cancer consultations. One village in Zamfara organized a viewing night every Friday. A university in Kano invited Halima to speak to their medical students about culturally sensitive care.

People no longer whispered, "that sick woman." Now they said, "Halima from TV- the brave one."

But the work took a toll.

There were filming days when Halima could barely sit upright. When her voice cracked. When makeup couldn't hide the sallow shadows beneath her eyes. But she pressed on. Because now, her voice was more than her own.

One evening, after shooting a segment on postsurgery healing, she had to be carried to the car. The nurse traveling with her wanted to cancel future shoots.

But Halima, breathing slow and shallow, whispered, "Let's film the next one from my house. I'll wear something bright. They need to see me smiling."

And they did.

That episode filmed on her porch, with chirping birds and neighbourhood children playing in the background became the most watched of the season.

By the year's end, ***"Halima Speaks"*** was picked up by national television and translated into three local languages. International health NGOs began to cite her model as a case study in community-led awareness. UNICEF sent a commendation. A Nigerian filmmaker announced plans for a biopic. Halima's name was mentioned in a global cancer care forum in Geneva.

But for Halima, the greatest reward remained the letters.

Folded notes from girls who wanted to become doctors. Messages from husbands who now accompanied their wives to screenings. Drawings from children who called her "Mummy of Strength."

Television had given her message wings.

And as her body grew weaker, her voice grew louder carried by frequencies, fibres, and faith.

Halima had always believed in the power of the spoken word, how stories could build bridges, heal wounds, and plant seeds of courage in hearts that had never dared to hope. But it wasn't until her words were carried by a television signal that she truly grasped their reach.

It started humbly.

A producer from a local Northern Nigerian TV station, Arewa Sunrise, had been watching Halima's work unfold from afar, her speaking engagements, her interviews, her open letters about cancer and silence in conservative communities. When he called, Halima thought it was a mistake.

"You want me… on television?"

"Yes, Hajiya," he said. "We want the real you. Not a celebrity. A mother. A teacher. A survivor who tells the truth with dignity."

The idea was simple: a weekly 30-minute health education program focused on cancer awareness, presented in Hausa and enriched with cultural sensitivity. But Halima's condition had changed. Her strength fluctuated. Fatigue often wrapped around her like a heavy shawl. Filming felt like an impossible dream.

Until Musa, her steady husband stepped in. "You've taught all your life, "he said gently.

"Now you'll just be teaching from a chair."

And so the show was born: "Halima Speaks: Truth, Health, and Hope."

The set was modest woven mats, embroidered cushions, calabashes on the shelf. The kind of home that felt familiar, comforting. Halima wore her colourful *abadas* and soft *gele (*tradition gown for men and, head gear for women*)* never overdone, always grounded. She didn't posture or preach. She simply spoke as one woman to another, as a mother to a daughter, as a survivor to someone still searching for answers.

She talked about the first time she felt pain and thought it was nothing. She explained what chemotherapy was, comparing it to *zafi da magani* - pain and medicine walking side by side. She invited guests: doctors from Zaria, survivors from Bauchi, faith leaders from Sokoto.

She tackled myths head-on.

"No, cancer is not a curse," she said one evening.

"No, it does not come from evil spirits."

"No, if you check early, you are not calling sickness to yourself, you are fighting for your life."

Viewers tuned in, sometimes dozens crowded around a single television set in a local viewing centre. In places where electricity was unreliable, communities shared power banks and solar panels just to catch her words.

Women wrote letters to the studio, folded in local fabrics and scented with *turaren wuta (incense)*, thanking her for the strength to speak to their husbands. Teenage girls sent her drawings. A group of nurses from a rural clinic started a WhatsApp group called *"Halima's List"*, a referral network inspired by her call to action.

Her reach expanded rapidly.

Arewa Sunrise's segment was picked up by NTA for a national health spotlight. Then came DSTV Hausa, where her episodes were rebroadcast across Africa. Clips were translated into Yoruba, Igbo, and even Pidgin English. International NGOs sponsored subtitled versions for the diaspora. Soon, Halima was being streamed in parlours in Kaduna, salons in Nairobi, homes in Birmingham, and even health education seminars in Washington, D.C.

She wasn't just a voice now. She was a phenomenon.

But behind the lights and lenses, Halima remained grounded. She insisted on shooting some episodes from her home, where children played in the background and the occasional chicken crowed outside the window. She believed the authenticity reminded viewers that health issues weren't foreign they were woven into everyday life.

Still, the work was hard.

There were filming days when Halima needed an oxygen mask between takes. Sometimes she couldn't speak for long without coughing. The crew adjusted setting up shaded rest areas, working shorter hours, scripting around her energy.

One day, after wrapping a segment on post-mastectomy recovery, Halima leaned back and whispered to the producer, "If I go tomorrow, let this message go farther."

And it did.

Her show became a reference in public health forums. University researchers in Ghana and South Africa cited ***Halima Speaks*** as a breakthrough in culturally grounded health education. UNICEF and WHO mentioned her work in health communication toolkits. A New York Times article called her “The Woman Who Taught a Nation to Listen.”

But for Halima, it wasn’t about headlines. It was about *her people*.

The market woman in Borno who got screened for the first time. The imam in Kano who opened Friday sermons with a message about cancer prevention. The schoolgirl in Niger who now wanted to be a radiologist.

Her voice had become a mirror a way for people to see themselves, not just as victims of circumstance, but as actors in their own health journeys.

And in homes across Nigeria, her closing words became a kind of prayer:

“Speak. Ask. Listen. You are not alone.

CHAPTER 6: What Remains

Halima always knew she was living on borrowed time. Not in a sorrowful way, but in a clear-eyed, purposeful one. Every sunrise felt like a whispered gift. Every breath, a gentle reminder: *You're still here. Say what must be said.*

By now, she had stopped asking for a cure. She asked instead for clarity, for grace, for time enough to leave instructions.

As her illness deepened, the camera crews grew more cautious. The episodes were spaced out. Her presence on-screen became more symbolic, short appearances, voice-overs, messages read by protégés. Yet her absence only seemed to magnify her message. Across Northern Nigeria and beyond, people watched old episodes with reverence. In some homes, ***Halima Speaks*** was treated like scripture.

She spent more days at home now, wrapped in soft cloths, the smell of cloves and *kunu* lingering in the air. Her children would sit beside her with notepads, recording her thoughts. Her voice had grown softer, but not her conviction.

She called each child in, one by one.

To her eldest daughter, she said: *"You are the fire beneath my feet. Don't let silence become your comfort. Speak even when your voice shakes."*

To her youngest son: *"Don't remember me as sick. Remember the laughter. The chalk on my fingers. The smell of new books."*

To Musa, her anchor: *"They will ask you how I did it. Tell them I didn't do it alone."*

One morning, she requested a camera.

The producers thought she wanted to film another episode. But she asked for something different - a farewell message. A soft curtain in the background, sunlight pouring in. She wore her favourite *zanna bukar* - indigo, embroidered with tiny silver beads. Her scarf was loosely draped, her cheeks hollow but glowing.

The camera rolled.

"I am not afraid," she began. "Because fear is not our inheritance. Courage is. And legacy."

She spoke not just of cancer, but of healing. Not just of survival, but of memory. She thanked those who listened. She blessed the young girls watching. She asked the nation to keep building clinics, asking questions, normalizing screenings, and listening to women.

And then, with a soft smile, she closed:

"If you remember me at all, let it be as a woman who chose to speak. And if you must remember my voice - let it be in your own."

She passed quietly, two weeks later.

The news broke across every major channel. "Nigeria Mourns Halima Yusuf." Tributes poured in - from presidents, traditional rulers, medical associations, survivors, schoolchildren. Streets were renamed. Murals painted. The airwaves hummed with her voice.

But the most powerful tribute came not from a headline, but from what followed.

Within months, The Halima Yusuf Foundation for Cancer Awareness and Women's Health was launched, spearheaded by her family and former colleagues. Based in Minna, it combined media outreach, mobile screening clinics, and community education hubs. The slogan was hers: ***"Speak. Ask. Listen."***

Her children carried the torch.

Zainab took over the coordination of *Halima Speaks*, now a broader platform featuring new voices, young survivors, rural nurses, female doctors. The show expanded into digital media, school curriculum supplements, and cross-border collaborations with East African networks.

Her son adapted her story into a children's book, ***Mummy's Quiet Fight***, which became part of a national curriculum on health education.

A mobile app launched in her name, into Hausa, Fulfulde, and Kanuri - allowing rural women to assess early symptoms and find nearby clinics.

International recognition came again, posthumously. A hall in the World Cancer Conference was renamed "The Halima Yusuf Dialogue Room." Her speech from Geneva was quoted in medical textbooks and policy papers.

But in Minna, in the neighbourhood where she once sat beneath neem trees and spoke to her neighbours, the true legacy lived on.

A girl knocked on the foundation door, holding her mother's hand.

"She has a lump," the girl said. "And we remembered what Halima said - 'Don't wait.' So… we came."

What remains of Halima Yusuf is not just memory. It is movement.

It is voice echoing through living rooms, hospital halls, and open skies.

It is a new generation, unafraid to ask. Unafraid to speak.

Because she spoke first

Epilogue: The Stage She Built

Ten years after Halima Yusuf's passing, her legacy lives on at the National Women's Health Conference in Abuja. Her daughter, Zainab, now takes the stage under the same skylight where Halima once stood. Holding her mother's old journal, Zainab speaks with pride and purpose, sharing Halima's story of courage and using it to launch new initiatives - including health clinics, a fellowship for young women in medicine, and an animated series based on *Mummy's Quiet Fight*.

A surprise farewell video from Halima moves the audience to tears, her message urging others to use their voices as she once did. Outside, a bronze statue of Halima beneath a neem tree symbolizes her nurturing strength. The epilogue closes with a powerful reminder: Halima didn't just raise awareness she raised a generation, and her voice still echoes in every act of advocacy that followed.

About the Author

Denise U. Ejoh, PhD is the CEO of the Cormode Cancer Foundation and founder of the Cormode Cancer Champions Club.

After launching the foundation in 2019, she has led bold, community-driven cancer awareness campaigns across Nigeria and the UK, blending culture, language, and lived experience into public health education.

A passionate advocate, she has authored books for young people including *Stronger Than Her Scars* and *Brave Hearts of Zuba* and produced over 100 educational videos aimed at empowering patients and the wider public.

Denise is also a familiar voice and face in cancer advocacy media. She hosts "Kakaaki Cancer Awareness" on AIT, "Cancer with Dr. Denise Ejoh" on PlusTV Africa, and the Zoom-based series "Let's Talk About It Cancer." Through these platforms, she continues to inspire early detection, treatment awareness, and survivor-led change, leaving a lasting impact on patients, students, healthcare professionals, and communities.

Printed in Dunstable, United Kingdom

68333801R00047